Fred.k Douglass

FREDERICK DOUGLASS
(1817 or 1818–1895)

QUOTATIONS

OF

Frederick Douglass

APPLEWOOD BOOKS

Frederick Douglass

FREDERICK DOUGLASS was born enslaved in Talbot County, Maryland. The exact date of his birth is unknown; Douglass believed he was born in the month of February, and he thought the year was 1818. He later chose February 14 as his birthday because, as he later told, his mother had called him her "little valentine." His mother gave him the name Frederick Augustus Washington Bailey, but he would change his name to Douglass when he successfully escaped slavery in 1838.

Around the age of twelve, Douglass received his first few lessons in reading and writing, illegally provided by his enslaver, Miss Sophia Auld, when he was living in Baltimore. This began Douglass's lifelong passion for learning.

Upon his escape from slavery at the age of twenty, Douglass quickly became a successful abolitionist, reformer, and one of the most recognized figures in nineteenth-century America. Along with the abolition of slavery, Douglass was also a champion for women's rights and was one of the few men to attend the first Woman's Rights Convention at Seneca Falls in 1848.

In the early part of his career, Douglass worked for William Lloyd Garrison's abolitionist newspaper, *The Liberator*. Beginning in 1847, he wrote, edited, and published a series of his own newspapers, starting with *The North Star*. When that folded in 1851, he would, over the next twenty-three years, publish, in succession, *Frederick Douglass' Paper*, *Douglass' Monthly*, and the *New National Era*.

Douglass wrote three books in his lifetime. *Narrative of the Life of Frederick Douglass: An American Slave* was published in 1845. The book became a bestseller and was influential in promoting the abolitionist cause. His second book, *My Bondage and My Freedom*, was also a huge success. His last autobiography, *Life and Times of Frederick Douglass*, was published in 1881.

After the Civil War, Douglass remained an active campaigner for civil rights for Freedmen and was a vocal proponent for giving African Americans the vote. At the end of Reconstruction in 1877, Douglass was appointed to several high-ranking federal positions, including minister resident and consul general to Haiti.

After a lifetime of social and political reform, Frederick Douglass died at his home in Washington on February 20, 1895. He was seventy-seven years old.

QUOTATIONS
OF
Frederick Douglass

*T*he silver trump of freedom had roused
my soul to eternal wakefulness. Freedom
now appeared, to disappear no more forever.
It was heard in every sound, and seen in
everything....I saw nothing without seeing it,
I heard nothing without hearing it, and felt
nothing without feeling it. It looked from
every star, it smiled in every calm, breathed
in every wind, and moved in every storm.

—*Narrative of the Life of Frederick Douglass:*
An American Slave (1845)

*Y*ou have seen how a man was made a slave;
you shall see how a slave was made a man.

—*Narrative of the Life of Frederick Douglass:*
An American Slave (1845)

I love the pure, peaceable, and impartial Christianity of Christ: I therefore hate the corrupt, slaveholding, women-whipping, cradle-plundering, partial and hypocritical Christianity.

—*Narrative of the Life of Frederick Douglass: An American Slave* (1845)

Fred. Douglass

*R*ight is of no sex, Truth is of no color, God is the Father of us all, and we are all Brethren.

—Douglass's motto for his weekly publication *The North Star*, 1847

*W*e are one people—one in general complexion, one in a common degradation, one in popular estimation. As one rises, all must rise, and as one falls all must fall. Having now, our feet on the rock of freedom, we must drag our brethren from the slimy depths of slavery, ignorance, and ruin. Every one of us should be ashamed to consider himself free, while his brother is a slave.

—"An Address to the Colored People of the United States," *The North Star*, September 29, 1848

*E*very blow of the sledge hammer, wielded by a sable arm, is a powerful blow in support of our cause. Every colored mechanic is, by virtue of circumstances, an elevator of his race. Every house built by black men, is a strong tower against the allied hosts of prejudice.

—"An Address to the Colored People of the United States," *The North Star*, September 29, 1848

*W*e might just here drop the pen and the subject, and assume the Constitution to be what we have briefly attempted to prove it to be, radically and essentially proslavery, in fact as well as in its tendency; and regard our position to be correct beyond the possibility of an honest doubt.

—"The Constitution and Slavery,"
March 16, 1849

Fred^k Douglass

*T*he white man's happiness cannot be purchased by the black man's misery. Virtue cannot prevail among the white people, by its destruction among the black people, who form a part of the whole community. It is evident that the white and black "must fall or flourish together."

—"The Destiny of Colored Americans,"
November 16, 1849

*W*hat, to the American slave, is your
Fourth of July? I answer: a day that reveals
to him, more than all other days in the year,
the gross injustice and cruelty to which he is
the constant victim. To him, your celebration
is a sham; your boasted liberty, an unholy
license; your national greatness, swelling
vanity; your sounds of rejoicing are empty
and heartless; your denunciations of tyrants,
brass-fronted impudence; your shouts of
liberty and equality, hollow mockery; your
prayers and hymns, your sermons and
thanksgivings, with all your religious parade,
and solemnity, are, to him, mere bombast,
fraud, deception, impiety, and hypocrisy.

—"What to the Slave Is the Fourth of July?"
Rochester, New York, July 5, 1852

*T*he only way to make the Fugitive Slave Law a dead letter is to make half a dozen or more dead kidnappers. A half dozen more dead kidnappers carried down South would cool the ardor of Southern gentlemen, and keep their rapacity in check.

—"The Fugitive Slave Law," *Frederick Douglass' Paper*, August, 1852

I would unite with anybody to do right; and with nobody to do wrong.

—"The Anti-Slavery Movement," 1855

We, the abolitionists and colored people, should meet [the Dred Scott] decision, unlooked for and monstrous as it appears, in a cheerful spirit. This very attempt to blot out forever the hopes of an enslaved people may be one necessary link in the chain of events preparatory to the downfall and complete overthrow of the whole slave system.

—Speech on the Dred Scott Decision, 1857

Frederick Douglass

The general sentiment of mankind is that a man who will not fight for himself, when he has the means of doing so, is not worth being fought for by others, and this sentiment is just. For a man who does not value freedom for himself will never value it for others, or put himself to any inconvenience to gain it for others.

—"An Address on West India Emancipation," August 3, 1857

*I*f the colored man can rise from degradation to respectability in Brazil, with the same treatment he can rise here. If he can be esteemed as a man by Portuguese, he can be so esteemed by Anglo-Saxons and Celts. If he can have justice at the hands of Catholics, why not also at the hands of Protestants?

—"Citizenship and the Spirit of Caste," May 11, 1858

Fred'k Douglass

*H*e [John Brown] believes the Declaration of Independence to be true, and the Bible to be a guide to human conduct, and acting upon the doctrines of both, he threw himself against the serried ranks of American oppression, and translated into heroic deeds the love of liberty and hatred of tyrants, with which he was inspired from both these forces acting upon his philanthropic and heroic soul.

—"Captain John Brown Not Insane,"
Douglass' Monthly, November 1859

*T*o suppress free speech is a double wrong. It violates the rights of the hearer as well as those of the speaker.

—"A Plea for Free Speech," Boston, December 10, 1860

Fred'k Douglass

*T*he Government is aroused, the dead North is alive, and its divided people united. Never was a change so sudden, so universal, and so portentous. The whole North, East and West is in arms. Drums are beating, men are enlisting, companies forming, regiments marching, banners are flying, and money is pouring into the national treasury to put an end to the slaveholding rebellion.

—"Sudden Revolution in Northern Sentiment," *Douglass' Monthly*, May 1861

*T*he American people and the Government at Washington may refuse to recognize it for a time; but the "inexorable logic of events" will force it upon them in the end; that the war now being waged in this land is a war for and against slavery; and that it can never be effectually put down till one or the other of these vital forces is completely destroyed.

—*Douglass' Monthly*, May 1861

*T*he destiny of the colored American... is the destiny of America.

—Speech at the Emancipation League, Boston, February 12, 1862

*A*ll but the willfully blind or the malignantly traitorous, know and confess that this whole movement, which now so largely distracts the country, and threatens ruin to the nation, has its root and its sap, its trunk and its branches, and the bloody fruit it bears only from the one source of all abounding abomination, and that is slavery.

—"The Slaveholders' Rebellion," July 4, 1862

*O*ur slaveholding rebels with an impudence only belonging to themselves, have sometimes compared themselves to Washington, Jefferson, and the long list of worthies who led in the revolution of 1776, when in fact they would hang either of those men, if they were living, as traitors to slavery, because, they each and all, considered the system an evil.

—"The Slaveholders Rebellion," July 4, 1862

*F*ree forever oh! long enslaved millions, whose cries have so vexed the air and sky, suffer on a few more days in sorrow, the hour of your deliverance draws nigh! Oh! Ye millions of free and loyal men who have earnestly sought to free your bleeding country from the dreadful ravages of revolution and anarchy, lift up now your voices with joy and thanksgiving for with freedom to the slave will come peace and safety to your country.

—"Emancipation Proclaimed,"
Douglass' Monthly, October 1862

*W*ho would be free themselves must strike the blow. Better even die free, than to live slaves. This is the sentiment of every brave colored man amongst us.

—"Men of Color, to Arms!"
Rochester, New York, March 2, 1863

*O*nce let the black man get upon his person the brass letters "U.S.," let him get an eagle on his button, and a musket on his shoulder, and bullets in his pocket, and there is no power on earth or under the earth which can deny that he has earned the right of citizenship in the United States.

—"Negroes and the National War Effort," Philadelphia, July 6, 1863

*S*lavery is not abolished until the black man has the ballot. While the Legislatures of the South retain the right to pass laws making any discrimination between black and white, slavery still lives there.

—Speech on the Thirteenth Amendment, May 1865

I hold that women, as well as men, have the right to vote, and my heart and my voice go with the movement to extend suffrage to woman.

—"What the Black Man Wants," speech in Boston, 1865

Fred'k Douglass

A thousand years hence, when the solid marble that held his remains shall have crumbled; when hundreds of military heroes who have risen under his administration shall have been forgotten; when even the details of the late tremendous war shall have faded from the pages of history... then Abraham Lincoln, like dear old John Brown, will find eloquent tongues to rehearse his history....Wherever freedom has an advocate, or humanity a friend, his name will be held as an auxiliary.

—"The Assassination and Its Lessons,"
Brooklyn Academy of Music, 1866

*T*he Constitution of the United States knows no distinction between citizens on account of color.

—"Reconstruction," *The Atlantic Monthly*, December 1866

A man's rights rest in three boxes. The ballot box, jury box and the cartridge box. Let no man be kept from the ballot box because of his color. Let no woman be kept from the ballot box because of her sex.

—Speech, November 15, 1867

*W*e have for a long time hesitated to adopt and carry out the only principle which can solve that difficulty and give peace, strength and security to the republic, and that is the principle of absolute equality.

—"Our Composite Nationality," Boston, December 7, 1869

$\mathcal{P}$ersonal independence is a virtue and it is the soul out of which comes the sturdiest manhood. But there can be no independence without a large share of self-dependence, and this virtue cannot be bestowed. It must be developed from within.

—"Self-Made Men," 1872

W.ᵐ Douglass

$\mathcal{Y}$ou say you have emancipated us. You have; and I thank you for it. You say you have enfranchised us. You have; and I thank you for it. But what is your emancipation?— what is your enfranchisement? What does it all amount to, if the black man, after having been made free by the letter of your law, is unable to exercise that freedom, and, after having been freed from the slaveholder's lash, he is to be subject to the slaveholder's shot-gun?

—Speech at the 1876 Republican National Convention, June 14, 1876

*T*he heart of the nation is still sound and strong, and as in the past, so in the future, patriotic millions, with able captains to lead them, will stand as a wall of fire around the Republic, and in the end see Liberty, Equality, and Justice triumphant.

—Speech delivered in Union Square,
New York, Decoration Day 1878

*W*hen I was about thirteen years old, and had succeeded in learning to read, every increase of knowledge, especially anything respecting the free states, was an additional weight to the almost intolerable burden of my thought, "I am a slave for life." To my bondage I could see no end. It was a terrible reality, and I shall never be able to tell how sadly that thought chafed my young spirit.

—*Life and Times of Frederick Douglass* (1881)

*M*en who live by robbing their fellow men of their labor and liberty have forfeited their right to know anything of the thoughts, feelings, or purposes of those whom they rob and plunder. They have by the single act of slaveholding voluntarily placed themselves beyond the laws of justice and honor, and have become only fitted for companionship with thieves and pirates—the common enemies of God and of all mankind.

—*Life and Times of Frederick Douglass* (1881)

*N*o man can put a chain about the ankle of his fellow man without at last finding the other enfastened about his own neck.

—Speech at Civil Rights Mass Meeting,
Washington, D.C., October 22, 1883

*T*he life of the nation is secure
only while the nation is honest,
truthful, and virtuous.

—Speech on the 23rd Anniversary of
Emancipation in the District of Columbia,
Washington, D.C., April 1885

Fredk. Douglass

*O*ur faith in him was often taxed and
strained to the uttermost, but it never
failed...we were at times stunned, grieved,
and greatly bewildered; but our hearts
believed while they ached and bled.

—Speech on the 21st Anniversary of
Lincoln's assassination, April, 1886

*T*he great fact underlying the claim
for universal suffrage is that every man
is himself and belongs to himself, and
represents his own individuality, not only
in form and features, but in thought and
feeling. And the same is true of woman.
She is herself, and can be nobody else
than herself. Her selfhood is as perfect and
as absolute as is the selfhood of man.

—Speech at the New England Woman
Suffrage Association, May 24, 1886

*M*y strongest conviction as to the future
of the negro therefore is, that he will not
be expatriated nor annihilated, nor will
he forever remain a separate and distinct
race from the people around him, but that
he will be absorbed, assimilated, and will
only appear finally, as the Phoenicians
now appear on the shores of the Shannon,
in the features of a blended race.

—"The Future of the Colored Race," May 1886

*R*aces and varieties of the human family appear and disappear, but humanity remains and will remain forever.

—"The Future of the Colored Race," May 1886

Fred. Douglass—

*W*hatever the future may have in store for us, one thing is certain; this new revolution in human thought will never go backward. When a great truth once gets abroad in the world, no power on earth can imprison it, or prescribe its limits, or suppress it. It is bound to go on till it becomes the thought of the world.

—Speech to the International Council
of Women, March 31, 1888

*T*he Abolitionists were right in their attitude to the Church. Slavery and the Church were side by side: the Church was at peace with slavery: men were sold to build churches, women sold to pay missionaries, and children sold to buy Bibles. We did right to oppose it.

—Speech at the Abolitionist Reunion in
Boston, September 22, 1890

Fred.ck Douglass—

*N*ow that the Union is no longer in danger, now that the North and South are no longer enemies: now that they have ceased to scatter, tear, and slay each other, but sit together in halls of Congress, commerce, religion, and in brotherly love, it seems that the negro is to lose by their sectional harmony and good will all the rights and privileges that he gained by their former bitter enmity.

—"The Race Problem," delivered before the Bethel Literary and
Historical Association, Washington, D.C., October 21, 1890

The true problem is not the negro, but the nation. Not the law-abiding blacks of the South, but the white men of that section, who by fraud, violence, and persecution, are breaking the law, trampling on the Constitution, corrupting the ballot-box, and defeating the ends of justice. The true problem is whether these white ruffians shall be allowed by the nation to go on in their lawless and nefarious career, dishonoring the Government and making its very name a mockery.

—"The Race Problem," delivered before
the Bethel Literary and Historical Association,
Washington, D.C., October 21, 1890

I have seen dark hours in my life, and I have seen the darkness gradually disappearing, and the light gradually increasing....And I remember that God reigns in eternity, and that, whatever delays, disappointments, and discouragements may come, truth, justice, liberty, and humanity will ultimately prevail.

—"The Race Problem," delivered before the Bethel Literary and Historical Association, Washington, D.C., October 21, 1890

Mr. Lincoln was not only a great President, but a great man—too great to be small in anything. In his company I was never in any way reminded of my humble origin, or of my unpopular color.

—*Life and Times of Frederick Douglass* (1892)

*I*t is not uncommon to charge slaves
with great treachery toward each other,
but I must say I never loved, esteemed,
or confided in men more than I did in
these. They were as true as steel, and no
band of brothers could be more loving...

—*Life and Times of Frederick Douglass* (1892)

*M*y subject is Haiti, the Black Republic;
the only self-made Black Republic in the
world. I am to speak to you of her character,
her history, her importance and her struggle
from slavery to freedom and to statehood.

—Lecture on Haiti, delivered at the World's Fair,
Chicago, Illinois, January 2, 1893

A hundred white men will attend a
concert of white negro minstrels with faces
blackened with burnt cork, to one who will
attend a lecture by an intelligent negro.

—"The Lessons of the Hour,"
Washington, D.C., January 9, 1894

Fred'k Douglass

*B*ut how can this problem be solved? It
cannot be done by repealing all federal
laws enacted to secure honest elections. It
can, however, be done, and very easily done,
for where there's a will, there's a way! Let
the white people of the North and South
conquer their prejudices....Let the American
people cultivate kindness and humanity.

—"The Lessons of the Hour,"
Washington, D.C., January 9, 1894

Fredk Douglass—